Cairns
Normanton
Townsville
Mt. Isa
QUEENSLAND
Rockhampton
Mt. Morgan
Longreach
Bundaberg
Maryborough
BRISBANE
Toowoomba
Coolangatta
SOUTH AUSTRALIA
Grafton
Woomera
Coffs Harbour
NEW SOUTH WALES
Broken Hill
Port Augusta
Port Pirie
Newcastle
Mildura
ADELAIDE
SYDNEY
CANBERRA
Bendigo
VICTORIA
Ballarat
MELBOURNE
Geelong
Bairnsdale
Lau ceston
ASMAN A
OBART

Beautiful Australia In Colour

Beautiful Australia In Colour

John Ross

Photographs By
Robin Smith, Michael Morcombe
and others

Lansdowne Press

LANSDOWNE PRESS
(a division of I P C Books Pty Ltd)
37 Little Bourke Street Melbourne 3000
First published 1970

Reprinted 1972, 1974
Typeset by Dudley E. King Melbourne
Printed and bound in Hong Kong
ISBN 0 7018 0308 8

Photographs supplied by
the Pictorial Library of Australia

Contents

Introduction

Australia—a great and ancient land mass, washed by three oceans and stretching almost from the equator to the roaring forties. A land of diversity, of contrasts and contradictions that mock the phrase 'typically Australian' and the untutored visions of rolling plains supporting gum trees, sheep, kangaroos and lean men with wide brimmed hats.

For here, too, are soft green hills, vine festooned jungles, densely forested mountains and snow covered peaks, the blazing red domes and pinnacles of ancient inland ranges, fertile coastal plains, millions of square miles of desert and sombre heathlands—an enormous scenic spectrum. While the greatest variety of scene lies close to the coasts, behind the mountains and forests and well bred geometry of agriculture is the brooding heart of the land, an eternal presence of ochre and earth colours, of fantastic alien shapes and an unbelievable monotony of desert and plain.

The band of highlands down the eastern flank of Australia, formed by a great wrinkling of the earth's crust many millions of years ago, is a vast carapace of broken tablelands and peaks. It shelters and waters the civilised east, provides its superb diversity of scenery and the richness and safety of its pastoral land.

This is home to most Australians, the city dwellers and the people of the closely settled rural areas. The three biggest cities, Sydney, Melbourne and Brisbane, sprawl across the lush coastal plain that pushes up sugar crops in the tropical north and rich grass for the pampered dairy herds of the south. To add to the blessing of the fortunate east the seaboard is indented with river estuaries and inland waterways, lined by thousands of miles of wide beaches and ennobled by rugged cliffs and headlands and, occasionally, mountains which stray from the range to meet the sea.

In the north it is flanked, too, by the Great Barrier Reef, a 1,200 mile long buttress of brilliantly-coloured coral heads and ledges, tropical and continental islands, clear, warm waters and an abundance of marine and bird life.

Behind the coastal strip the mountains thrust and roll in blue hazed grandeur, densely clothed, sometimes in lush rainforest but mostly in smaller eucalypts and acacias, cut in the more spectacular regions by ravines, gorges and escarpments, pouring water to the coast in short, sharp rivers and down to the more gradual landward slopes into lazy brown rivers which wind, gum lined through rich plateau lands. But gradually the rivers dry up and are replaced by wandering channels that become rivers only after heavy rain, the trees space out until, finally, they become a rarity. The red desolation of the outback takes over, cut by great saw toothed ridges and towering masses that are like no other mountains on earth. Then, more than 1,500 miles west, the coastal pattern in reverse rolls green lands into the Indian Ocean.

This huge physical spectrum is host to an enormous range of unique and distinctive animal life. There are over 150 marsupial animals which carry their young in inbuilt cradles, among them the kangaroo and koala, the emblems of Australian wildlife, and the Tasmanian 'Tiger', one of the rarest animals in the world. There are the egg laying mammals, antiquated rarities, the echidna and the platypus. The kookaburra's droll laughter is the friendliest and most recognisable sound from within an incredible variety of bird life. Shy lyrebirds, rewarding the patient with a glimpse of their beauty in the southern forests, soaring wedgetailed eagles, dancing brolgas, emus and parrots—all have lent individuality to Australia.

But the most unremitting factor in the Australian landscape is the gum tree. In its many guises and varieties it is the scenic link in the Australian vastness. Perhaps monotonous en masse, but each with an individual strength and beauty, these living representatives of a distant past have survived and thrived in Australia. The smell of eucalyptus is so much the essence of rural Australia that it can bring tears to the eyes of sophisticated expatriates.

Australians have brought their country, in less than 200 years, from the mists of antiquity to a leadership among nations. They have tamed the land and made it work for them; they have forged great industrial development from natural resources that are, as yet, only marginally exploited; they have built great cities and achieved one of the world's highest living standards; they have, for a country of 12 million people, made a big impact in the arts, in science, in industry and in sport.

But this is a book, not of people, but of their background—the Australian country and coastline. It is a book which has aimed at capturing and delineating the beauty of the land and its infinite variety, the backdrops before which the busy drama of Australian life is being played.

New South Wales

The beautiful city of Sydney thrusts and arches itself around a fine confusion of bays and inlets. Its towers of commerce and white sailed opera house gleam down into the waters of the breathtakingly beautiful harbour. It sparkles back, seemingly unsullied by the constant passage of ferries, ocean going ships, workboats and other maritime miscellany. On weekends it becomes white canopied with the sails of a thousand yachts.

Overhead the great iron bridge rumbles with the chronic indigestion of big city traffic, pouring cars in and out of the colourful, bustling canyons of the city.

This is Australia's oldest, biggest and most fascinating city. It is sprawling, lusty, sometimes grimy, always noisy, but it has, on the whole, made the most of its beautiful setting. Its waterside houses peep down through their gardens to tranquil inlets lined with pleasure craft; city workers look up from their desks to see ocean liners gliding through the harbour; the coastal suburbs to the north and south fringe eighteen miles of golden surf beaches—Manly, Dee Why, Avalon, Palm Beach, Coogee, Maroubra.

The city, still vaguely Victorian in architectural atmosphere but undergoing an immense facelift, throbs with cosmopolitan life. Its northern and coastal suburbs spread over steeply scarped sandstone hills cleft with ridges of rock. To the south and south-west its industries spread in a grey and grimy ring that pumps life into the commercial arteries from 16,000 factories.

Its nightlife, centred on the legendary Kings Cross, is lively, loud and attractive; its culture vigorous and *avante garde;* its citizens friendly, outgoing and sport crazy.

This is the heart of New South Wales, the most populous State with 4,430,000 people, and the leading primary, mineral and manufacturing producer.

The other major industrial areas are black spurs on the green flank of the coast. Newcastle, 100 miles north of Sydney, is a coal and steel city and the seaboard heart of the rich Hunter Valley. Wollongong-Port Kembla, 50 miles south of Sydney, is the main heavy industry city in Australia.

The State encompasses hundreds of miles of ocean beaches, beautiful river, lake and mountain scenery, an expanse of harsh, flat interior plain, a sub-tropical north coast, and a belt of snow covered highlands in the south.

The topography falls into the four natural north-south divisions common to the eastern states: the narrow and fertile coastal plains, the tablelands of the Great Dividing Range, 30 to 100 miles wide and rising to high mountain regions in the north and south, the undulating western slopes of the range and the dry plains of the far west.

Some of the State's most interesting and beautiful country lies within 50 to 150 miles of Sydney—country like the Hawkesbury and Nepean River District, the Illawarra Coast, the Blue Mountains and Jenolan Caves, and the southern highlands, with their historic towns and homesteads.

Closest to the city, in the north, is the magnificently rugged Ku-ring-gai Chase, 40,000 acres of dense sandstone bushland abounding in wildlife. It abuts one of the finest waterways in the world, Broken Bay and the lower reaches of the Hawkesbury River.

One of the most delightful and peaceful holidays in Australia is a 'skipper yourself' cruise on the clear sheltered waters of Broken Bay's three branches—Pittwater, Brisbane Water and Cowan Creek. The banks are heavily timbered and rock walled, broken by secluded sandy spits, valleys and winding inlets that demand exploration.

The Hawkesbury region was once the granary of the infant settlement of Sydney. Its upper reaches, which become the Nepean River, flow through the historic towns of Richmond, Windsor and Penrith, where some of the finest examples of Colonial architecture are preserved.

At the head of Brisbane Water is the picturesque town of Gosford, and a little further north are the Tuggerah Lakes—three sheltered lakes separated by narrow spits which lead to the resort towns of The Entrance, Toukley and Budgewoi.

The Blue Mountains, beginning about 40 miles west of Sydney, are, from a distance, an intense cobalt blue. Spectacular sandstone precipices ring the densely wooded valleys and the rugged terrain is broken by deep gorges. The mountains are well settled—a favourite holiday and retirement region. The biggest tourist attraction is the Jenolan Caves, Australia's most spectacular limestone caves, elaborately lit so that tourists can see the fantastic forms and subtle colours of the calcite deposits.

South of Sydney is heavily timbered mountain country, dominated by Mt Gibralter and Mt Jellore and enclosing areas of rich farmland, the second food production area for early Sydney. One of the older towns here, Berrima, with its fine sandstone buildings, has been preserved as it was in the nineteenth century.

The seaward peaks of the highlands look down on the Illawarra coast, an incongruous mixture of heavy industry centred around Wollongong, sweeping surf beaches and beautiful resort towns, like Shell Harbour, Kiama and Ulladulla.

Sydney's holiday makers also flock to the far south coast, where the seaboard is punctuated by a series of small resort towns set around lakes and waterways and a string of surf beaches.

Behind the coastal strip is the Kosciusko State Park—the Australian alps—a magnificent amalgam of lakes, streams, mountains, forests and heathland. The giant among the mountains is Mt Kosciusko, Australia's highest mountain at 7,314 feet, but much of the region is snow-covered for six months of the year and supports the country's most popular and well developed ski resorts at Thredbo, Perisher Valley and Smiggin Holes.

Conducted tours of the Snowy Mountains hydro-electric project attract thousands of visitors every year. This huge project has harnessed the waters of the Snowy River System to provide power for Sydney and Melbourne and irrigation for 1,000 square miles of farmland. It has involved the building of 600 miles of roads through previously inaccessible country, and nine major dams. Access to the mountains has benefited skiers, fishermen—Lake Eucumbene has perhaps the best trout fishing in the country—and nature lovers, who can see here an abundance of wildflowers in summer and a great variety of temperate zone plant and animal life.

The Snowy Mountains are the watershed for the Riverina, the unspectacular but attractive and highly productive south-central region. It is a solid part of the State, with a pleasant and reliable climate, well settled land and prosperous cities and towns like Albury, Deniliquin, Wagga Wagga, Gundagai and Yass. High yields of wheat, fine merino fleeces and the rice, fruit, wine and table grapes of the Murrumbidgee Irrigation Area are economic mainstays of the Riverina. It merges to the north with the central west, rolling wheat and wool country on the western slopes of the Great Dividing Range and centred around Orange, Dubbo and Bathurst, which became Australia's first inland settlement when Governor MacQuarie chose its site in 1815.

The north-western region of the State is more scenically exciting. In the east, as the land sweeps down from the tablelands of New England, are the dramatic outcrops of the Warrumbungle and Nandewar Ranges, impressive mountains with precipitous gorges and rock faces. In the west is black soil wheat country and the new cotton country on the Namöi River flat near Narrabri. From the western flat lands the country stretches into the largest area of highland in Australia, New England, where 900 square miles lies above 3,000 feet. New England is more closely settled than most mountain regions of Australia, so travellers who appreciate good roads and facilities can also enjoy a richness of scenery—heavily wooded mountains, gorges with long cascades and waterfalls, panoramas of forests and rivers, and rich, cultivated valleys. New Englands 'capital' is Armidale, the seat of the University of New England, the Armidale Teachers' College and similar establishments and the nearest thing in Australia to a 'university town'.

A surge of tourism must surely come to the north coast, the still rural strip between New England and the sea. It is laced with rivers like the Mackay, Nambucca, Bellinger, Richmond and Tweed, flowing through forested valleys into the flood plains of the coast. The climate is hot in summer and gentle in winter, the surf beaches are still peaceful and the sea, river and estuary fishing hard to better. The big inland towns of Taree, Kempsey, Lismore and Casino are likely to one day play second fiddle to resorts like MacQuarie Harbour, Coffs Harbour, Camden Haven and Nambucca Heads.

New South Wales, like all the mainland States, finally stretches into the great Australian inland. The far west of New South Wales is little more friendly than the other inland regions, and has no fascinating formations of land to relieve it. It is a red monotony of plains, broken by low rocky ranges, sluggish, twisting rivers and, very occasionally, civilisation. But it is not all wasteland, as it carries over two million merino sheep and great mineral riches. Here is Broken Hill, the biggest inland city in Australia and isolated home of 31,000 people—the workers of the silver, lead and zinc mines of the Barrier Range and their families. They have carved a progressive city out of sun beaten wilderness, and sustain settlement and bright parks and gardens with a main water supply from the Darling River dam, 20 miles west.

Following Federation of the Australian States in 1901, the Constitution provided for the establishment of a Seat of Government on a site in New South Wales. An area of highland on the western slopes of the Great Dividing Range was chosen and in 1909 was transferred from State to Commonwealth jurisdiction. This tract of land of 911 square miles, with an additional 28 square miles at Jervis Bay, now constitutes the Australian Capital Territory. Here stands Canberra, the Federal capital of Australia, 200 road miles south-west from Sydney and 400 road miles north from Melbourne.

Conceived and developed as the nation's capital it has had the advantage of total and enlightened planning which has made it both the most formal and most handsome of Australian cities. Visitors complain of its cold, impersonal atmosphere, but there is beauty and stimulation in the magnificent public buildings and an aesthetic nicety of order and spaciousness in its suburbs.

The city is superbly situated in an undulating amphitheatre of the Australian Alps, bisected by the Molonglo River, which has been dammed to make Lake Burley Griffin. The lake gives the city grandeur and a centre of focus. Parliament House and the new National Library look across it to the war memorial and the commercial centre on the northern shore.

Canberra is Australia's fastest growing city, with a population of 110,000. To cope with a projected increase to 250,000 by 1984 satellite cities of Woden and Belconnen have been planned. The city has become a tourist 'must' and over 600,000 non-official visitors come each year to see parliament in session, the war memorial, the academy of science, the national library, operations at the mint, the 258 ft. aluminium spire of the Australian-American memorial, the Australian National University, the Mt Stromlo Observatory, 10 miles out, and the space tracking stations of Honeysuckle Creek and Tidbinbilla.

But this is a ritual sightseeing, largely devoid of the stimulus of the unexpected. Beautiful, haphazard Sydney, with its restlessness and pulsating life far better represents a country's strength and its surge of progress.

The Macleay River near Kempsey on the north coast of New South Wales.

Cattle droving in northern New South Wales.

Right The 3,800 foot peak of Mt Warning dominates the surrounding Tweed River landscape in northern New South Wales. Surrounded by rain forest, the peak was named by Captain Cook as a reminder of rocks close to Tweed Heads.
Below Lion Island and Pittwater at the mouth of the majestic Hawkesbury River just north of Sydney.

Impressive grandeur of the Snowy Mountains.

The Three Sisters, best known landmark of the Blue Mountains, at Katoomba.

Right Aerial view of one of Sydney's best-known surf beaches at Manly.
Below Breakers roll in at Harbord beach north of Manly.

Parliament House, Canberra, Australian Capital Territory, designed by Walter Burley Griffin, built in 1927.

Right The Banana Bowl area around Coff's Harbour on the Pacific Highway 361 miles north of Sydney.
Below Deua River country, south-eastern New South Wales.

Tasmania and Victoria

Tasmania and Victoria share the bounty and caprice of South-Eastern Australia's temperate climate; they are spurred and saddled with the sharp beginnings of the continents long Great Dividing Range and clothed with highly productive green lands and with great forests; they are the two smallest and most densely populated states.

But these facts in common bely the great differences in physique and character that place apart the States that face each other across the shallow and turbulent waters of Bass Strait.

Victoria, the most highly industrialised and populous state in the continent, is big in power and wealth. It takes up only three percent of the national area but carries 28 percent of the population (3,384,000 people) and makes or grows a third of the gross national product. The value of its factory production has risen by over $1,200,000,000 in five years, its primary output is increasing, it has the world's largest brown coal deposits, and has now added oil and natural gas to its resources.

The island of Tasmania is the smallest, least populated (388,500) and slowest growing State. Its total production is approximately 10 percent of that of Victoria. It is pinning its hopes for economic growth on increased industry spearheaded by such projects as the Savage River Iron Ore project, the Bell Bay Aluminium plant near the second city of Launceston, and on its energetic drive for tourists.

The two capitals, Melbourne and Hobart, demonstrate the differences in scale.

Melbourne is bland and urbane in mood, a city of the world that accepts its size and the onset of internationalism calmly. It easily absorbs glasshouse office towers into its broad streets and amongst the ornate buildings of its formative years.

Suckled on wheat and wool, nurtured by industry, accustomed to solid and well founded progress it remains the hub of Australian finance and the headquarters of industrial giants such as B.H.P. Pty. Ltd., Conzinc Rio Tinto and I.C.I. (Aust.)

Its $2\frac{1}{4}$ million people continue to spread in an affluent and conformist suburbia which extends 20 miles or more from the city and is bounded in the east by the Dandenong Ranges and in the south by Port Phillip Bay, the almost landlocked expanse of water that is the city's main playground and route to the Port of Melbourne.

Despite its increasing architectural inconsistency Melbourne remains handsome and dignified. Situated on the Yarra River it is devoid of any outstanding natural feature, but is enlivened by its magnificent parks and gardens, which are held inviolate, by authority and public insistence, from the slightest ravage of progress. The formality of its gardens has led to its reputation as being the most 'English' of the Australian capitals, and perhaps its solidity and conservatism help to give some credence to this judgement.

Hobart seems less a capital city and more an old sea-port town. It faces the Derwent Estuary and the wild southern ocean, its landscape dominated by the bulk of forest clad Mt Wellington. Its waterfront, once the lusty home port of the southern whaling fleet and centre of Australia's biggest shipbuilding industry, has a picturesque and historic charm which refuses to succumb to an overgrowth of modernisation. The city has many fine Georgian homes and old buildings, such as the Gothic Holy Trinity Church and whaler's cottages at Battery Point, or the magnificent line of bond-stores down at Salamanca Place.

Opposite Lake Albina, almost at Kosciusko's summit lies at the brink of a tremendous river gorge. Beyond rise the blue ridges of the Geehi Walls.

New building development has scarcely diminished the nineteenth century character and atmosphere of the city proper, and the unhurried and formal manner of its commercial life. Hobart's suburbs, expanding now across a Derwent spanned by the superb Tasman Bridge, are planned to maintain a spacious, semi-rural atmosphere and the undulating country on both sides of the estuary enables a fine individuality of house siting and design. If Hobart people have anything to complain about in their environment it is their winter weather.

Tasmania, the highest rainfall State, is more green and lush than the mainland. Nowhere in the verdant valleys and flat lands of the island is one out of sight of blue hazed ranges or mountain peaks.

The terrain is dominated by the Great Central Plateau, the fountain of a big hydro-electric scheme. With peaks rising above 5,000 feet, and broken by river valleys, the plateau increases in ruggedness from east to west, ending in the thick western forest country. The south-west is so dense and inaccessible that thousands of square miles have yet to be explored on foot. It is ribbed with ravines bearing rushing rivers, and webbed in parts by the 'horizontal' (anadopetalum) plant that makes passage virtually impossible.

The unsurpassed grandeur of the whole mountain and forest region of the west was once equalled only by the difficulty of getting anywhere near it. Until 1932, when a road was forced through the mountains between Queenstown and Hobart, the lonely mining towns in this ore rich region were connected with the world by ships small enough to enter MacQuarie and Triall harbours on the indented and sea battered shoreline.

The savage magnificence of the region, softened at times by the brilliance of flowering heaths and shrubs in the more open country, presents an amazing contrast with the rich and gentle valleys of the Derwent and Huon estuaries in the south-east.

This is where nearly all southern Tasmanians live, and where the bulk of the island's apple and fruit crops are grown. At the headwaters of both rivers are the hardwood forests which feed the newsprint industry at New Norfolk; stretching east and north are flatter lands which are noted for their production of high quality wools.

The Tasman and Forestier Peninsulas in the east shelter Hobart from the Tasman Sea and here, in a setting of rolling pasture lands and towering cliffs and capes, are the grim echoes of convict days in the elegant ruins of Port Arthur and Eaglehawk Neck, where once a chained line of bloodhounds barred the way of escaping felons. The east coast, traversed by the Tasman Highway, has the island's most equable climate and is the main tourist and holiday region. The coastline, from Triabunna south to Tasman Head, contains hundreds of miles of sheltered waters ideal for boating, fishing and water sports. Tourism is increasing rapidly, but farming, fishing and timber getting remain the basis of the east coast economy.

The richest agricultural land in Tasmania is the northern coastal plain between the central mountains and Bass Strait. Launceston, 40 miles from the coast at the junction of three rivers, is the 'capital' of this densely-settled region; a pleasant, quiet provincial city built around a series of hills and connected with the coastal towns by the Bass Highway and with the port and industrial area to its north by two highways which flank the Tamar estuary.

The northern coastline is rather featureless, but the charm of the north lies in its gentle pastoral landscapes, traversed by many small clear streams and with distant vistas of snow clad peaks and ridges. In the mountain country behind the plain there is the fantastic vertical rock formation of the Great Western Tiers, and the Cradle Mountain—

Lake St Clair National Park, the largest sanctuary and scenic reserve in Tasmania. This wild confusion of mountain ranges is snow-capped most of the year, with its scenery reflected in glacier carved, rock walled lakes.

From Launceston to Hobart the 124 mile Midlands Highway runs through gentle farmlands. The midlands were settled early and fine old mansions, barns, farm-houses, inns and bridges—often convict built, give the region a beautiful and timeless quality, with European oaks, willows, poplars, elms and briar and hawthorn hedgerows making a brilliant autumn display.

Tasmania's bush carries over 200 species of birds, some peculiar to the island, unique varieties of plants and two of the world's rarest animals, the Tasmanian 'Devil', a bear-like mammal, and the Tasmanian 'Tiger', a lone hunting marsupial wolf.

Scenically Victoria presents a virtual microcosm of the vast diversity of Australian landscape. Within its borders are contained semi-arid plains, scrubby desert, monotonous sweeps of flat pasture land, rich and rolling farm country. Its uplands enclose long and gentle valleys, and there are snow capped mountains, sparkling beaches and lonely stretches of rugged coast, tumbling mountain streams and lazy green-brown rivers.

As the southern spur of the Great Dividing Range dominates Tasmania, the western end crops up in western Victoria and it sweeps across the State in a widening arch which carries through to the Victorian Alps in the north-east and reaches laterally into Gippsland and the north-central region. About 900 square miles of the high country is snow covered from June to October and is sparsely forested with twisted and delicately barked snow gums. The mountains are accessible through the north-eastern uplands and the ski resorts attract tens of thousands of people to the chalets and lodges of Mt Buller, Mt Hotham and Falls Creek, built in the dark wood and stone style of the Tyrol, which maintain a comfortable and sophisticated high-life around the ski-runs.

The Great Dividing Range is the catchment area for the Murray River which forms the State's northern boundary and the rivers which, running north through central Victoria and south through Gippsland, feed the State's most productive agricultural, dairying and fruit growing land.

The north-east also benefits from a wide irrigation system. The cities of Shepparton in the Goulburn Valley and Wangaratta in the Ovens Valley are handsome thriving centres, an example of the prosperity of many Victorian towns from a mixed primary and manufacturing economy. At the same time other big towns throughout Victoria have relatively static economies as they wait for the benefits of industrial decentralisation away from the capital.

On the other side of the divide Gippsland curves around the east coast and up to the State border. Its climate is pleasant, but with a high rainfall to water the State's richest dairying and cattle country and the wild eastern mountain regions which are the base of big timber industries. The heart of Gippsland, and the electrical power centre of Victoria is the Latrobe Valley, where vast brown coal deposits are mined by open cut and big industrial-rural towns spread out under the smoke of the power plants. Further east the Gippsland Lakes stretch in 150 square miles of waterways, sheltering behind the wild, ocean pounded stretch of the Ninety Mile Beach and giving focus to a growing tourist area. Jutting out from South Gippsland is the beautifully desolate headland of Wilsons Promontory, a national park and protected resort, and the southernmost point on the Australian mainland.

But the most popular resort areas of the State are nearer Melbourne. The picturesque hill towns of the Dandenong ranges blend with the dense cover of tall mountain timber, lush plant life and autumnal brilliance of introduced European trees to attract bush-walkers and day trippers like a magnet. This is the home of the lyrebird—a rare and beautiful bush songstress.

Mornington Peninsula, a boot-shaped promontory between Port Phillip and Western-port Bay is *the* summer place—jampacked in January and with holiday homes stretching in a 40-mile line from Frankston to Portsea along the edge of Port Phillip Bay.

In the west the Bellarine Peninsula, near Geelong, gives way to a rugged coastline, and here the Great Ocean Road, twisting between coastal cliffs and wooded ranges, leads to the beach towns of Lorne and Apollo Bay.

Geelong, 40 miles from Melbourne is Victoria's second city, a port and manufacturing town of 110,000 people which styles itself 'the gateway to the Western District'. From it the Pacific Highway runs into the comparatively featureless plains of the south-western corner of the state—plains bordered by a lonely coastline of golden cliffs and high, wave-cut spires, arches and gorges, and in the east by the rocky Grampians, an isolated mountain chain. The Western District, as it is miscalled, is grazier country, carrying a third of the State's sheep and beef cattle population and, as a centre of the rural Establishment, studded with some of the finest mansion homesteads in the land. Its main cities are the deepwater port of Portland and the thriving coastal town of Warrnambool.

The central-west is hot, flat and dry country—the Wimmera—where the bulk of Victoria's cereal crops are grown and which gives way to the scrub haunts of the mallee fowl. Inland from it is the pastorally and industrially varied central region, unspectacular country where the big, old towns of Bendigo and Ballarat look back to the more exciting days of the gold rushes which founded them.

North of the Wimmera lies the semi-arid Mallee, where the sandplains respond sufficiently to rainfall to produce a big wheat crop. Technically in the Mallee, too, is the Murray irrigation area around Mildura, intensively cultivated farmlands which produce a bounty of citrus orchards, vineyards and olive groves. The Murray Valley region winds with the river across the north, rich in mixed farming and beginning to reap the benefits of tourists to its river reaches and clear, sunny climate—the most stable climatic region of a State that, for all its wealth and advantages, is notorious for its unpredictable weather.

The Grampians of western Victoria have a unique beauty. They were named by the explorer Major Mitchell because they resembled the Grampians of his native Scotland.

View from gorge, Mt Buffalo in the Australian Alps, 200 miles north of Melbourne.

Right One of Victoria's largest and most popular national parks is at Wilsons Promontory, a mountainous peninsula where massive granite headlands shelter wide sandy beaches.
Below The Yarra River and the skyline of the city of Melbourne.

Mt Buffalo, one of Victoria's most popular snow resorts in the Australian Alps. The 5,645 foot peak rises above an isolated granite plateau in the Mt Buffalo National Park.

Right Autumn leaves at Bright on the Ovens River in the shadow of the Australian Alps.
Below Wave-cut cliffs and residual spires at Port Campbell on the south-western coast of Victoria.

Mellow beauty of hop fields landscape in the Valley of the Derwent River, Tasmania.

Right The ruins of the church, Port Arthur, on the southern coast of Tasmania. Built of stone and with tower and spire, it was calculated to hold 1,200 people on the ground floor.
Below The Tasman bridge across the Derwent River at Hobart.

Right Stormy seas surge against the cliffs of a coastal scenic reserve near Eaglehawk Neck on the Tasman peninsular.
Below Landscape on the King River, western coast of Tasmania.

Flower beds line the banks of this section of the Huon River, southern Tasmania.

Queensland

Queensland is a giant State, 1,300 miles long and 900 miles wide, the second-largest State in the Commonwealth—and the giant is awakening now as the enormous potential of its natural resources is being brought under control. It is a romantic land, holding an irresistible attraction for travellers in its winter sunshine, its reef fringed semi-tropical and tropical coast and beautiful eastern mountains.

But its riches are coming from many sources—from the huge coalfields of Central Queensland, once left untapped because of distance from markets but now highly valued by Japanese industry; from the raw bauxite mined at Weipa on the remote Cape York Peninsula and refined into alumina at Gladstone, the central coal port; from Mt Isa, the fabulous copper, silver, lead and zinc producer on the western plains, 600 miles inland from its northern port of Townsville; from the rock phosphate deposits of the north-west; from the oil and gas fields of the south-east; from the clearing of brigalow scrub country in the Fitzroy Basin of Central Queensland, which will increase beef production there by 350 percent; from the new beef roads of the distant western and northern cattle country; from the water conservation programme which will put to work some of the water that has run uselesssly from the land.

There is continued wealth, too, in its grain, wool, beef and mutton, sugar, fruit, daily products, cotton, peanuts, fish, tobacco, timber. And its growing manufacturing industry, still based mainly on the capital city of Brisbane.

Brisbane, lying around the Brisbane river in the south-west corner of the State, cannot hope to carry the weight of an enormous state on its shoulders. The big towns, like Gladstone and Rockhampton, Townsville and Cairns on the coast, and the small centres in the far west are more the commercial, cultural and social 'capitals' of their region than are the country towns of the smaller states.

But Brisbane is the effective centre of State control, the main port, the commercial and industrial heart of Queensland. It is a semi-tropical city with its suburbs thinly spread over hill country and its older houses built for the uncomfortable humid summer climate—an unattractive but effective style of timber bungalows on stilts with lattice screens, shutters and corrugated iron roofing.

The city itself is like a big country town, slow moving and easy going with narrow streets, verandahed footpaths and relatively few high rise towers among its old buildings. It is the most architecturally unimpressive of the State capitals, but its sub-tropical parks and gardens, its semi-rural suburbs and its warm climate help to make an attractive environment.

Brisbanites also have Australia's playland on their doorstep. The City of the Gold Coast, 50 miles away, is a 20 mile coastal strip of beautiful beaches, inland waterways and man made razamatazz. This is honeymoon country, the winter haven for wealthy southerners and a year round sunbaking, surfing and swinging tourist phenomenon. It is the second fastest growing city in Australia, after Canberra, with 60,000 permanent residents and room for 110,000 overnight visitors in its American-style, pool-fringed motels and high rise apartments. The main centre is Surfers Paradise, a never-sleeping concrete and neon town of bistros, bars, restaurants, snack counters and chic shops filled with a restless tide of

Opposite Majestic eucalypt on the Helenvale Road near Cooktown on the north-eastern coast of Queensland.

holidaymakers. It is a town of the bikini, of surf beaches drenched with pop music, of beer and hamburgers or gourmet dinners, of low tariff luxury. Behind the Gold Coast, and giving it a scenic dimension, lies the Mt Lamington National Park in the MacPherson Range. This is some of the most beautiful mountain and rainforest country in Australia, and is a delight for those who want to escape from the highlife below.

The Gold Coast starts a chain of coastal holiday land. Further north the Sunshine Coast combines its superb beaches and mountain backdrop with a more idyllic and peaceful atmosphere. This long string of beach and fishing resorts has bays, lakes and landscapes to give more variety of form and colour, but its hinterland lacks the grandeur of the Gold Coast mountains. The central coast, with its amazingly equable climate, and the north, which suffers hot and humid weather and 'the wet' between October and March, have their own attraction, but are seen by many tourists as a jumping off point, from Rockhampton, Mackay, Townsville and Cairns, for the islands of the Great Barrier Reef.

The 1,250 mile long reef is the largest coral conglomeration in the world, carrying over 300 varieties of spectacularly beautiful coral, mostly submerged. Its warm, clear waters are studded with densely vegetated coral cays and islands and support a great range of seabird and marine life, including brilliantly-hued tropical fish.

The resort islands varying in style from luxury accommodation to simple cottages and lodges, have been popularised both by their perfection of setting and package tours which have made them more accessible and inexpensive. Most reef islands are isolated portions of the continent, like the Whitsunday Group, a dreamlike configuration of islands containing six reef resorts.

More than half of Queensland lies above the Tropic of Capricorn. Physically it has four main regions—the coastal strip, the eastern highlands of the Great Dividing Range, the western tableland country and the vast western plains. Between them they provide an infinite variety of scene, from the lush jungle of Cape York to the bare, parched lands of the west.

With heavily forested mountains as a constant backdrop the northern coastal strip carries mile after endless mile of sugar cane crops, green as they grow and rising to a great golden thatch of maturity. During the harvesting season roaring fires light the night as the cane is burnt before cutting. The strip is narrowest in the north and south, reaches far inland in some places and in others, where the mountains impinge upon the sea, is replaced by long inland valleys, such as the Bowen-Proserpine corridor. Some land is of sandstone formation, terracotta ground of open forest country, but the alluvial valleys of the river flats are supremely fertile.

The coastal north is unsurpassable in its beauty, with its flowering tropical trees and mountains rising out of the meandering, sugar planted flat lands. The drive from Cairns to Port Douglas on a winding coast road flanked by mountains and quiet bays must rank as one of the most pleasant experiences in Australian travel. Further north is explorer country, the jungle country and wilds of the Cape York Peninsula.

The mountain belt is at its most rugged and spectacular in the north and south, where the peaks are closest to the sea. South of Cairns Mt Bartle Frere and Mt Bellenden Ker lift their wooden crests above 5,000 feet—moody mountains, sometimes capped in billowing white or lowering grey cloud, sometimes lost in the fury of a tropical rainstorm. There are many other tourist spectaculars in this northern region—at Ravenshoe the Tully Falls are beautiful and eerie in the roar and sheer fall of their waters; the railway from

Cairns to Kuranda winds through the mountains, climbing 1,000 feet in 12 miles and leads to the Barron River Gorge, the longest fall of water in Australia, but now only released after heavy rain. The Gillies Highway from the tabeland down to Cairns is an alpine road in the tropics.

Further south is the progressive city of Mackay, the centre of Australia's largest sugar-growing district and the point of departure for a number of Barrier Reef and island cruises. The port of Mackay is one of the largest artificial harbours in Australia and its bulk sugar loading terminal is the largest in the world.

Fifty miles west of Mackay is Eungella 'Land of the Clouds'; with its 120,000 acres of highlands it is one of Queensland's best-known and most spectacular national parks, protecting the rainforest country of the Clark Range.

The Glasshouse Mountains, 50 miles north of Brisbane, thrust their sharp heads above forest and bushland, a group of ancient thracyte volcanoes with eight principal peaks of convoluted spires, domes and pillars. Captain Cook gave them their name because they reminded him of the glasshouses of his native Yorkshire.

The Tablelands to the west are rolling, open country with placid, gum-lined rivers. The Darling Downs in the south and the Atherton Tablelands of the north are big areas of highly productive black soil country, famous for its bloodstock studs, the Darling Downs also produces most of the State's grain and fruit. It is rural Australia at its best, attractive in its proximity to the eastern mountains, with well laid out and prosperous towns and well-kept national parks and sanctuaries. Its commercial centre, Toowoomba, the largest inland Queensland city, has a fine climate and an attractive environment of wide, tree-lined streets and beautiful public parks and gardens.. It is the road and rail junction serving the south-western pastoral areas, the Moonie oilfields and the Roma gasfields.

On a plateau between the Burdekin and Palmer River headwaters, west and south of Cairns, lies the volcanic land of the Atherton and Evelyn tablelands. This relatively isolated and unpopulated dairying and agricultural region has its own beauty in its rocky hills, rolling land and surrounding mountains.

The big, sparsely populated, isolated and harsh country of Queensland is the Western Plains, a great savannah of 320,000 square miles of semi-arid rolling downland, interspersed with flat topped hills and tablelands. It survives and supports a large pastoral industry, because of the greatest artesian basin in the world, which has been tapped by deep bores for stock and domestic supply. Here are the winding watercourses of the south-west channel country, usually dry but capable of flooding into a great sheet of water which flows into the salt pans of the central deserts. In the north-west the 500 mile long Mitchell River drains 47,000 square miles of territory as it flows into the gulf of Carpentaria.

The towns of the west—Roma, Cunnamulla, Longreach, Winton, Cloncurry—are small, but they take on an importance as a lifeline to civilisation for the outback Queenslanders. Mt Isa is a town apart, with its population of over 18,000, its model town amenities, houses, shops and sports facilities, its man-made Lake Moondarra, its rodeo which brings rough riders from all over Queensland and its immense mining installations.

Mary Kathleen, near Cloncurry, is another model town, built for uranium miners and their families, but empty now as its rich ore is kept 'in storage' awaiting a market.

The inner west boasts one of the most unusual national park reserves in Australia—the Carnarvon Ranges; rough and broken, with deep, narrow sandstone gorges, overhangs and caves, many of which contain 'galleries' of Aboriginal rock paintings and engravings. The spring wildflowers of the Carnarvons are prolific and brilliant.

Queensland encompasses an abundance of rare plant, animal and bird life—cassowaries, brush turkeys, brolgas and birds of paradise; cuscus possums, pigmy gliders and rabbit bandicoots; flame and firewheel flowering trees and rare forest varieties of kauri, hoop and bunya pine, Queensland maple and silkwood, bush box and native tamarind—life as rich, varied, and at times exotic, as the State that supports it.

Right Heron Island, a low coral cay surrounded by reefs that extend northwards 12,000 miles to New Guinea.

Pentecost Island in the Whitsunday Passage off the Central Queensland coast, seen from Lindeman Island.

Right Aerial view of Surfers Paradise, one of Australia's most popular tourist resorts.
Below From Highway One near Ingham there is an impressive panorama across tidal flats, mangrove swamps and channels to mountainous Hinchinbrook Island.

Tropical beach scene at Newell, northern Queensland.

The Centre

In the centre of Australia is a red rock, rising in primordial majesty 1,143 feet above a wide sandy flat plain which is covered in spinifex and desert oak; the rock is two and a quarter miles long, one and a quarter miles wide. As the sun plays on it during the day it changes colour through shades of fiery red to delicate mauve. Occasionally rain falls and veils it in a silver torrent which runs into the waterholes and desert beneath, like icing on a cake for some gargantuan feast. This is Ayers Rock. People who hardly know of Sydney and Melbourne have heard of it. It is the supreme tourist attraction in a country full of them, a life sustaining force in an ancient and barren land.

There are other places too—The Olgas, Kings Canyon, Gosse's Bluff, the Organ Pipes, Ormiston Gorge, Palm Valley, the Valley of Eagles, the Dancing Girls—fantastic places formed by the cataclysms of another age. But Ayers Rock surpasses them all. Each year thousands of visitors travel by plane and four-wheeled-drive vehicle 250 miles from Alice Springs to see it, and to explore the eroded caves in which the Aboriginals of long ago tribal days have left galleries of rock paintings. They see the Sound Shell, a cavity as smooth as if formed by the sea; the Brain, a wall eroded and honeycombed into the shape of a human brain; the Kangaroo Tail, a 500 foot strip of stone hanging down one end of the Rock. Like a file of ants the visitors climb the western end to the summit, a wide expanse of stone dotted with scraggy bushes and trees.

From here they have a clear view west to the centre's second wonder—the Olgas. This is a cluster of rounded massive rocks rising from the spinifex plain, as dramatic and vividly coloured as the Rock, but lacking the majesty of its great bulk. The tallest of the Olgas, Mt Olga itself, is 1,790 feet above the oasis-like Valley of the Winds which runs through the rock system.

These most spectacular of the ancient, eroded rock formations of the centre are also furthest away from the tourist 'capital', Alice Springs. Nearer at hand are the many starkly beautiful rock and mountain formations, cliffs, gorges and valleys of the MacDonnell Range system.

Over the centre is a brooding and forbidding challenge of unremitting harshness, silence and immensity. But 'The Alice', gateway to a forgotten age, is very much of the present. The rough buildings and dusty, potholed streets of pioneering days are gone, and in their place is an attractive, well maintained town of wide, tree-lined streets, modern houses, smart arcades, art and curio shops, restaurants, hotels and motels. These are the trappings of a multi-million dollar tourist industry which has supplanted trucking and cattle farming as the town's main source of wealth. In a winter of superb, cloudless weather upwards of 40,000 people use the town as a base for exploration of the wonders of the centre. Through the town runs the Todd River, one of the winding watercourses of the centre which are usually dry but are capable of rising to flood after freak heavy rain. In Spring the 'Henley on Todd' Carnival is one of the highlights of the year at 'the Alice', with the enthusiastic competitors carrying their boats down the dry river bed in a parody of big city regattas.

The best of the scenery which draws the tourists to the area lies west of Alice Springs, where the Finke and other rivers have cut chasms and gorges into the stark chains of mountains. Closest to the town are Heavitree Gap, Simpson's Gap and Standley Chasm,

Opposite Wind-whipped dunes create a scene of savage beauty in the Great Sandy Desert, far north of Western Australia.

where cliffs 200 to 250 feet high and only 12 to 18 feet apart leap into colourful life as the sun reaches into them near midday.

Further out are the Ellery, Serpentine, Glen Helen and Ormiston Gorges. Ormiston is the greatest of them, its cliffs rising hundreds of feet from the clear still waters of Ormiston Creek, and its rock faces changing colour as the day advances. Near Glen Helen, where the Finke River passes through the range are Window Rock, Stonehenge, and the strange vertical strata known as the Organ Pipes. The backdrop to this region is Mt Sonder, rising 4,400 feet and the most distinctive of the central mountains, which march in long and eerily symmetrical lines across the land. To the south-west of Mt Sonder is Gosse's Bluff, a circle of eroded hills enclosing a crater said to have been formed by the crashing of a meteorite.

The Finke River course runs down past the Hermannsburg Aboriginal mission and a monument to the famous artist of the centre, Albert Namitjira, and into Palm Valley. This is the loveliest valley in the centre, an oasis in a deep walled gully with many beautiful waterholes. Here and in the nearby Glen of Palms is the solitary refuge of the *Livistona mariiae* tree, a tall graceful palm, and the shorter stemmed cycad palm. The valley, a flora and fauna reserve, abounds in wildlife. Like Glen Helen it has a modern tourist lodge set in a circle of rocks known as the Amphitheatre. The rocks have been named according to their shape—Sundial Rock, Cathedral Rock, Battleship Rock and Corroboree Rock.

Kings Canyon, in the George Hill Range, 160 miles south-west of Alice Springs, has only recently been opened to visitors. It is a massive cleft of deeply-coloured rough-hewn walls with an oasis of deep rock pools, cycad palms and ghost gums at its head.

The centre is the lower region of the Northern Territory which has an area of 523,000 square miles and a total population of only about 40,000 white Australians and Aboriginals.

The link between Alice Springs and Darwin, the administrative capital of the territory on the north coast, is the Stuart Highway, a 1,000 mile long ribbon of bitumen that does something to allay the traveller's sense of isolation. It is a fascinating journey through some of the loneliest country in the world, with the traveller much more likely to see cattle, kangaroos, wild donkeys, buffalo and wild pig than people. The highway runs out of the red country of the centre into the wide plains covered by low eucalypt, acacia scrub and hardy semi-desert grasses. Here beef cattle roam the open range on huge landholdings of up to a million acres.

Further north is the 'wet' country, low lying heavily-wooded plains which receive monsoonal rains but are poor grazing land. They reach up, broken by mountains in the north-east, to the heavily indented north coast.

Ten miles north of Ti-Tree is a cairn to commemorate the naming of Central Mount Stuart, which stands brooding a few miles off the road in the faint purple haze so typical of the centre. The explorers John McDouall Stuart and William Kekwick named it Mt Sturt in 1860, but the name was later changed to honour Stuart. The explorers calculated that the summit of the mountain was the exact centre of Australia.

Further north are The Devils Marbles on both sides of the Stuart Highway; miles of gigantic rounded granite boulders, sometimes balanced precariously on top of one another, appear in scattered heaps which appear to have been hurled down by a giant hand.

The main centres on the road are Tennant Creek, 313 miles north of Alice Springs, a mining town which is growing as new fields are being opened, and Katherine, 220 miles south of Darwin, prosperous centre of the best grazing country in the territory.

Near the town is the Katherine Gorge, where the clear river flows between towering walls to form one of the most spectacular river canyons in Australia. The great cliffs are brilliantly coloured, and their natural beauty is enhanced by Aboriginal paintings in ochre high up on the rocks. The tropical country of the 'top end' has links in its vegetation with the Indo-Malaya-China region. Here is the banyan tree, with its mass of exposed roots, the bottle shaped, water storing baobab, and on the coast tamarinds, mangoes and pandanus palms. The ground is studded with strange fluted mounds, anthills that reach 14 feet high.

Despite the regular rainfall there is little nutriment in the land, 'the wet' has leached much of the good out of the soil and, although the speargrass grows up to 10 feet high, it is too rank and sour for stockfeed. Attempts to establish agriculture in the north have so far been defeated. The high hopes of the dry are drowned in the downpours of 'the wet'. The latest enterprises are large scale sorghum growing at Tipperary Station, and scientific pasture improvement experiments which may yet make the land more profitable for cattle.

As in 'the centre' tourism is the fastest growing industry in Darwin. This port and administration town is home for 26,500 territorians. For a predominantly public service centre it is remarkably unconservative—a lively and noisy town where beer is consumed in great quantities to combat the heat and where mildly eccentric behaviour passes unnoticed.

Darwin is built on a peninsula on the eastern shores of Port Darwin, a deep inlet of Clarence Strait, which runs between Bathhurst and Melville Islands and the mainland. It has been transformed in recent years from a fairly dilapidated outpost into a modern and well planned town with some fine public buildings, street plantations and parks and gardens.

Its summers are fairly humid and unpleasant, but the dry winter season is delightful. Apart from its climate there is fascination for the tourist in the wild life and vegetation of the tropics, and in a mangrove and palm fringed coastline that is deeply indented by the estuaries of large rivers.

Darwin is the jumping off point for crocodile, buffalo hunting and fishing 'safaris', and for trips to the 31,000 square mile Arnhem Land Aboriginal reserve in the north-east, or to the Rum Jungle uranium mines, the sorghum project and the experimental farms around Humpty Doo station to the south.

While the country around 'the Alice' has more to engross the dedicated 'sightseer' and photographer, Darwin and its surrounding country offers more variety and activity for naturalists and sportsmen.

Aerial view of the MacDonnell Ranges looking like rows of trenches fashioned by some giant of the past.

The beauty of the Centre after rain: mass display of wildflowers at Palm Valley, with Sundial Rock looming in the background.

Right Standley Chasm, a cleft in the Chewings Range west of Alice Springs. Near midday the walls leap into colour as the sun strikes down 250 feet.
Below The smooth ramparts of the Olgas about 20 miles west of Ayers Rock.

Ayers Rock crouches like some prehistoric monster on the flat surface of the desert. Twenty miles away in the background are the Olgas, another phenomenon of the Centre.

The Olgas, a jumble of huge domed boulders about 20 miles west of Ayers Rock. The tallest, Mt Olga, rises 1,790 feet from the surrounding plain.

Western Australia and South Australia

To many outsiders Western Australia might well be a collection of red, bare mountains full of iron ore, an island floating on oil, a series of holes in the desert which give forth nickel at the turning of the industrial faucet. With, of course, a pretty, sundrenched city in between for the dreamed of holidays from the stock exchange profits of this remote mineral wealth.

The names of Mt Tom Price, Mt Newman, Kambalda and Kalgoorlie, Goldsworthy Mining, Hamersley Iron, Barrow Island, Western Mining and Poseidon leap out of the world's finance pages—and, in truth, the great mineral projects have been the big factor in the rocketing rise of Western Australia from 'ugly sister' to 'girl of the golden west'.

But these new giants are mere pockmarks on the face of a huge, empty, harsh and hostile country—a State comprising roughly a third of the Australian mainland which softens its gigantic face only in the coast country of its south-western corner. And they tell only part of the story of Western Australia's big leap forward.

There is, too, the agricultural 'miracle' of the opening of the Esperance land in the south, the promise of the new beef roads and the Ord River cotton scheme in the lonely north. There is the culling of the splendid hardwood forests, wool, wheat, dairying and fruitgrowing, new factories and refineries, a diversity of production from salt and fertilisers to canned peaches, wine, pearls and prawns—all this and so much more.

Most of Western Australia's life and wealth still revolves around the south-west. Over 600,000 of the State's 930,000 people live within the statistical district of Perth, and most of the rest live in the south-eastern region. This doesn't leave many people for the rest of the State, but it is not country that treats people kindly. With the exception of the tropical Kimberley region in the north of the State, any point east of Kalgoorlie, is virtually uninhabited desert. The 600,000 square mile north-west is two-thirds desert and, despite iron ore exploitation, the Pilbara has a population of less than 20,000, many of them living a 'suburbia in the wilderness' existence in company towns like Mt Tom Price, Dampier and Wittenoom.

Patches of fantastic, alien beauty leap out of the featureless terrain of the north-west. The hundreds of miles of red sand, funereal mulga scrub and grey spinifex that wash over the country in a seemingly limitless ocean make the discovery of the strange, exciting forms and colours of tabletop mountains and peaks a doubly enriched experience. The 200 mile long Hamersley Range is enthralling in its starkness and swift changes of mood. The great weathered mountains, brightly stained by leached minerals, can break suddenly into delightful gorges, like Wittenoom and Yampire, holding still, clear and inviting pools. Further inland is the Chichester Range and the Isabella and Gregory Ranges, with their deep red mesas and canyons.

Cape and Rough Ranges, on the north-west cape, enclose enormous canyons and caves decorated with Aboriginal art. The eighty mile beach sweeping up to the one big and cosmopolitan town of Broome, is one of the world's finest and most lonely stretches of sand.

The desert gives way to the mountainous, timbered Kimberleys—open range cattle country where, here and there, big rivers like the Fitzroy, Ord and Lennard have cut deep channels through the ranges. The most spectacular is Geikie Gorge, where a great

Opposite Limned against the sky like a sentinel, an armed Aboriginal warrior watches from a vantage point in the MacDonnell Ranges.

pool is bordered by cream and chocolate banded cliffs.

The north's wild sublimity of scenery has been made more accessible by regular air services, but more travellers are braving the indifferent and bad roads for private tours of discovery.

From the coastal town of Carnarvon onwards the bitumen of the North-West Coastal Highway ends and they are ineradicably 'in the rough'. Carnarvon is on the perimeter of the more populous and comparatively more productive country of the south. It is the centre of the Gascoyne pastoral area, which is declining in productivity because of over-grazing and erosion. Now prawning and irrigated fruit and vegetable farms on the Gascoyne River, and the nearby NASA space tracking station, are the mainstays of the town's prosperity.

Southwards is the Murchison Coast and hinterland, scenically uninteresting away from the coast, but highly productive agricultural and pastoral land. Its port town of Geraldton, prosperous and well planned, attracts holidaymakers to its beaches, its superb winter climate, and the fishing around the offshore Abrolhos Islands.

The Geraldton Highway runs 312 miles south, through some of the west's best farming land, to Perth, the fastest growing capital in Australia. A city in transition—wracked by the sound of the jackhammer, distorted by a forest of giant cranes, gleaming with the architectural dentistry of new buildings—but still beautiful.

Once it lay dreaming by the Swan River, accustomed to the slow pace and peacefulness of a big country town. A new excitement and bustle has thrust upon it a more urgent and cosmopolitan air, an awakening social and cultural life, and great pride of achievement. Perth's port city of Fremantle, 12 miles downriver, is the first port of call for migrant vessels, and new arrivals who 'jump ship' there are making a good choice. For Perth has a reputation as a warm and welcoming place and is a clean, ordered and beautiful city, edged with riverside parkland and the overlooking expanse of Kings Park, 1,000 acres of natural bushland. Its climate, the best of any Australian capital, encourages a year round outdoors life of barbecues, beaches, boating and sport. Its major industry is concentrated away from the city, to the south and west, and at Kwinana, once an expanse of barren sandhills but now destined to become one of Australia's great industrial complexes.

Off the coast is Perth's holiday island of Rottnest—a low lying island which offers the simple attractions of sand, sun and a rich marine and land life. The Dutch seamen who named the island 'Rats Nest' thought its rare marsupials, the Quokkas, were giant rats.

The Darling Ranges to the south-east of Perth are ablaze in spring with thousands of varieties of wildflowers. This is just part of Western Australia's famous wildflower carpet, which spreads over millions of acres of the southern regions.

Karri and jarrah, with their durable and handsome timbers, are the prized trees of the timber glades of the south-west; tall and sombre forests which break into pastoral land and onto a coastline of lonely surf beaches and rocky shores.

The 60 mile stretch of country between Cape Naturaliste and Cape Leeuwin, at the extreme south-western tip of the continent, contains some beautiful limestone caves, many of which have only been partly explored.

The main towns of the south-west are the ports of Bunbury, 117 miles from Perth, and Albany, 254 miles south, beautifully sited on a deep, protected inlet and a short distance from the strangely sculptured Porongorup Ranges.

Further east, and 590 road miles from Perth, is the fast growing coastal town of Esperance —the centre of a region of three million acres which is being transformed by the 'miracle' of scientific land improvement. Land that, only ten years ago, was entirely useless for agriculture and almost useless for grazing is now producing prolific cereal crops and sheep pasture. The monotonous plains of Esperance break onto a coastline of wide lonely beaches and bold headlands, but Esperance's place as a summer holiday resort for the people of the interior has been overshadowed by its rising importance as the port for the new farming province and for the nickel mines around Kalgoorlie and Norseman on the western margin of the Great Victoria Desert. These sunblighted mining towns are the last outposts on the Eyre Highway which runs through the featureless Nullarbor Plain and, with the Indian Pacific Railway, links Western Australia with South Australia and its sister states in the east.

South Australia is the least endowed of the Australian States. Its northern two thirds is desert or semi-desert country, low on water and generally low on terrain. Its eastern third is rich and well watered but the west, on the other side of St Vincent Gulf and Spencer Gulf, peters out past the Eyre Peninsula into desert again.

The northern plains are either sandy or covered by gibber (small, weathered rocks) with big lakes, like Lake Eyre, which look nice on the map but contain water only after big rains in their catchment areas to the north and east.

The main mountain system runs from Kangaroo Island, at the head of Vincent Gulf, and the Yorke Peninsula, 500 miles northward. It includes Mt Lofty, the backdrop to the capital city of Adelaide, and the Flinders Ranges, which present some of the best mountain scenery in Australia. The changing colours of the gorges, spurs, valleys and towers as the light plays on them give the ranges a rare individuality that delights increasing numbers of visitors. The most visited region of the ranges is Wilpena Pound, where the great cliffs enclosing the valley are white at the tops, red-brown below and set in purplish shale. The Flinders region is clothed in parts with native pines and wattles and with huge red gums along creek beds, and in spring by a lush and breathtakingly colourful display of wildflowers.

The Mt Lofty Ranges near Adelaide rise abruptly from the coastal plain, wooded on their steeper slopes, planted with European trees and cultivated in the valleys. They are well populated but still pleasantly rural and are their most beautiful in spring and autumn. Adelaide spreads out below, on the Torrens River between the Gulf of St Vincent and the Mt Lofty Ranges. Like most Australian capitals it has suffered growing pains, but it retains a spacious atmosphere and a dignified, unhurried air. It is called 'the city of churches' and is certainly notable for its beautiful and well-preserved commercial and public buildings and for its parks and gardens. It is reputedly a stuffy and socially stratified city, led by an upperclass establishment, but a radical change of licensing laws has given it a more lively and spontaneous atmosphere. Its biennial Arts Festival is Australia's major cultural event.

Adelaide's industrial area stretches between the commercial city and the Port of Adelaide, on Largs Bay, nine miles north-west. The rapid growth of industry has also led to the establishment of Elizabeth, a satellite town of 35,000 people, many of them English migrants, and designed on modern town planning principles.

To the north-east of Adelaide is the Barossa Valley, the most important wine growing area of Australia. It is a gently beautiful thirty mile long valley of vineyards, olive groves, orchards and solidly permanent towns and wineries, built with care and the architectural influence of the homeland by the valley's Lutheran settlers.

The Murray, South Australia's only major river, flows on the eastern side of the main mountain chain, into the coastal lakes of Alexandrina and Albert. North of the Barossa the Murray River district runs to the Victorian border, a rich region of vineyards, orchards and irrigated farmlands, tranquil river scenery and reserves teeming with water birds.

The Victorian border and the southern ocean bound the south-eastern district, a picturesque region which carries large plantations of radiata pine. Its main centre of Mt Gambier takes its name from an extinct volcano holding four deep and very beautiful crater lakes. The best known is the Blue Lake, 600 feet deep and with walls 275 feet high, which changes colour from slate grey in winter to bright blue in summer.

South of Adelaide, where the Mt Lofty Ranges run down to the sea, the fine surf beaches and coastal scenery combine with green lands and lakes and fens teeming with waterfowl to make a beautiful holiday region.

On the other side of the St Vincent Gulf is 120 mile long, boot-shaped Yorke Peninsula, undulating and lightly soiled country used mostly for grain farming. The south of the peninsula is sparsely populated, but is attracting tourists to its peaceful sea-side towns and sunny climate.

The peninsula's western flank is bounded by Spencer Gulf, which cleaves into the coastline to the industrial city of Whyalla and to Port Pirie and Port Augusta. At the mouth of the gulf lies Kangaroo Island—70 miles south of Adelaide, 56 miles long and 25 miles wide. With its rugged coastline and waters teeming with fish it is becoming a popular holiday island. It has also undergone a transformation with the application of fertilisers and trace elements to the formerly useless scrublands of the interior.

The Eyre Peninsula is a dry, flat and hot land between Spencer Gulf and the Great Australian Bight, an important wheat growing district and with iron deposits in the north to supply the Whyalla foundries. In the south is Port Lincoln, a wheat port and the first of the fishing towns like Ceduna and Streaky Bay, that take great hauls of whiting and tuna in the seas off the magnificent south-western coastline.

Opposite Aroona Valley in the Flinders Ranges which begin about 120 miles north of Adelaide.

Cape Wiles on the Eyre Peninsula on the central coast of South Australia.

Right Vineyards at Seppeltsfield in the Barossa Valley.
Below Serene skyline of the city of Adelaide.

Right Sunrise on the distant walls of Wilpena Pound in the Flinders Ranges.
Below Aerial view of the renowned blue lakes at Mt Gambier. Four small lakes—the most beautiful of which is the Blue Lake—lie inside an ancient volcanic crater. During summer the Lake becomes an intense azure-blue.

The remarkably formed Wave Rock
at Hyden, Western Australia.

Right Bare granite domes of the Porongorups, a small range in the south-west of Western Australia, 20 miles south of the Stirling Range; Karri forests, with tall graceful trees cover the slopes.
Below The Narrows Bridge and Kwinana freeway, Perth.

Australia in Facts and Figures

Australia is the flattest continent in the world, with an average elevation of only 1,000 feet above sea level, compared with a world average of 2,300 feet. Almost three-quarters of the island continent is an ancient plateau, the Great Western Plateau, averaging about 1,000 feet. Another large division is the central eastern lowlands, extending north-south with an average height of less than 500 feet. Even the eastern highlands have only an average altitude of less than 3,000 feet, and no peak rises above 7,500 feet.

It is the driest continent—about 70 percent of Australia has a rainfall of less than 20 inches a year, nearly 60 percent received less than 15 inches and about 40 percent less than 10 inches. The total annual run off of Australian rivers is less than the St Lawrence River in North America. The greatest surface run off is from tropical Australia, and it is a hopeful indicator of future development that the northern water resources are practically unharnessed, while the waters of the south are substantially committed for use in hydro-electricity and irrigation projects. Australia lacks the extensive inland river systems of the mountainous continents, its largest system being the Murray River and its tributaries, but there are artesian bores under 60 percent of the continent which support stock on the arid inland plains.

Australia's size (2,964,741 square miles), global siting (straddling the Tropic of Capricorn) and physical features give it a varied climate. Slightly more than half of Queensland, 33 percent of Western Australia and 81 percent of the Northern Territory lies within the torrid zone. Central and southern Queensland are sub-tropical and further south are the warm, temperate regions of New South Wales, South Australia and Western Australia and the cooler areas of Victoria, south-west Western Australia and Tasmania.

Australia's claim to be a land of sunshine is borne out by the average daily hours of sunshine for the capital cities: Darwin 8·4; Perth 7·8; Brisbane 7·5; Canberra 7·2; Adelaide 6·9; Sydney 6·7; Melbourne 5·7 and Hobart 5·6. The mean temperatures of the hottest and coldest months in the capitals are: Darwin 85·3 (77·1); Brisbane 76·9 (58·7); Perth 74·6 (55·4); Adelaide 73·4 (51·9); Sydney 71·6 (53·3); Canberra 68·3 (41·7); Melbourne 67·7 (48·9); Hobart 61·7 (46·2).

In most areas January is the hottest month, although in Tasmania and Victoria February is hottest and in the tropical north, because of the increased cloudiness of the wet season from December to March, temperatures are highest in November.

In the drier inland the range of temperatures from early morning to afternoon increases with the distance from the coast. During the hot summers of the northern inland temperatures often go over 110°F. The most consistently hot area is inland from Port Hedland, Western Australia, where at Marble Bar from October 1923 to April 1924 there were 160 consecutive days with temperatures rising to at least 100°F.

The average annual rainfalls of the capitals, and the number of days on which rain occurs, are: Darwin 60·48 (97); Sydney 47·75 (150); Brisbane 44·89 (124); Perth 34·89 (121); Melbourne 25·83 (141); Hobart 24·83 (163); Adelaide 20·77 (121).

In the north, mainly on the eastern seaboard, forests and vegetation are those of the moist tropics. Further south, east of the Great Dividing Range particularly, the vegetation is of the warm temperate zone. Inland the progressively drier elements restrict growth to

Opposite Fortescue Falls, Dale's Gorge in the Hamersley Range, north-west Western Australia.

the river fringes, and there are extensive treeless areas.

Australia's long isolation as a landmass has resulted in a vegetation predominantly different from the rest of the world. The relatively arid conditions which came to prevail intensified the struggle for existence and led to the development of a large range of plant life adapted to the environment. These plants form the main part of Australia's flora, with eucalypts and wattles predominating.

Eucalypts have about 500 species. They thrive in cold or heat, wet or dry, the richest soil or infertile sand. The most majestic species are the Victorian mountain ash, the tallest hardwood in the world, and the karri and jarrah of Western Australia. Eucalypts provide nearly all of the general purpose hardwoods, and much of the country's paper.

Wattles (acacia) are pod-bearing plants, represented in Australia by over 600 species. Australia also has thousands of species of wildflowers. Each state has its own large range of endemic groups, with Western Australia the most lavishly endowed.

Australia's wildlife is remarkable for the presence of many unique animals and the absence of several orders known in other countries. The severance of land bridges with other continents left Australia as an island sanctuary for its large population of marsupials, which produced a differentiation of many types.

Nearly half of the approximately 230 species of mammals recorded in Australia are marsupials. The remainder comprise the placental mammals and the rare species of monotremes. These are the only egg-laying mammals known and are considered by some zoologists to be descendants from ancient forms which evolved from mammals to reptiles.

The platypus is a living fossil; a furred creature which lays eggs, suckles its young, has webbed feet and a ducklike bill. It inhabits the watercourses of eastern Australia. Spiny ant-eaters are land dwellers, they carry a protective coat of spines and have a tubular snout and long narrow tongue for catching ants and other insects. When alarmed they use their spade-like claws to dig into the ground, and on soft ground they appear to sink into the earth.

Marsupials vary markedly in size and general appearance—they range from kangaroos exceeding 6 feet in height to insectivorous species smaller than a house mouse. Throughout their wide diversity of habit and environment they share a common feature—the possession of a pouch to accommodate the young.

As well known as the kangaroo, and perhaps even more popular, is the koala, a solemn and inoffensive tree dweller which lives on the leaves of certain species of Eucalypt. Other tree-dwelling marsupials include the cuscus of the tropics, tree-climbing kangaroos and many types of possums. The relatively few carnivorous marsupials include insect-eating 'mice', large native cats and the Tasmanian 'Devil' and Tasmanian 'Tiger'. The 'Tiger' is almost a legendary creature, believed by some naturalists to survive still in the wild parts of Tasmania.

The dingo, a wild dog, is believed to have evolved from Asiatic dogs which accompanied the ancestors of the Australian Aboriginal on their migrations by sea. Australia's range of native placental mammals is restricted to species of rodents and bats, while marine mammals include whales, seals and the dugong, or sea cow.

There are about 700 bird species in Australia, with some 530 species considered to be endemic. It is the home of 60 known species of parrots and 70 species of honeyeater. The best-known birds are those of unique characteristics or beauty and include the beautiful, superbly vocal lyrebird, the black swan, the emu, the cassowary, the stately brolga, the kookaburra, the mound-building brush turkey, mallee fowl and scrub fowl, the Cape

Barren Goose, and the bush callers—whipbirds, bellbirds and magpies.

Reptiles include over 200 kinds of lizards, 140 snake types, two crocodiles, freshwater tortoises and marine turtles.

Australia's main mineral deposits are in two broad regions—The Precambrian rocks of Western Australia and South Australia, Northern Territory and parts of Queensland and New South Wales contain most metalliferous deposits—iron, lead, zinc, silver, copper, uranium, nickel and gold.

The mineralised Palaeozoic and Mesozoic rocks—containing gold, now mostly worked out, a few large areas of copper, lead, silver, zinc, and smaller amounts of other metals—extend round the east of the continent. Most of Australia's known black coal occurs in the eastern states, while there are large deposits of brown coal in Victoria. Significant oil and natural gas discoveries have been made at a number of places throughout Australia.

Mineral and farm products have always constituted the bulk of Australia's exports, and today they account for about 80 percent of exports. While the rural sector of the economy has been relatively static, the treasure house of mineral wealth uncovered in the last ten years has brought a new era of industrial and economic development.

Australia has become one of the world's biggest exporters of iron ore, mostly from reserves of at least 15,000 million tons of high grade ore in the north-west ranges, the Hamersleys and Opthalmias. The latest boom is in nickel, where what could prove to be the world's biggest deposits have been found at Kambalda in Western Australia. Bauxite, from Weipa in Queensland, is another new mineral to add to the silver, lead, zinc and copper extractions that have been the mainstay of Australian mining.

Manufacturing now employs some 1·3 million people—in over 60,000 factories. The greatest growth has been in metals, chemicals and engineering, and, on a population basis, Australia is now as highly industrialised as the United States.

Wool is still the greatest source of rural wealth. Australia produces about 30 percent of the world's wool, and the industry exports about 90 percent of its clip to provide about 30 percent of all export receipts. Beef and veal exports are only exceeded by Argentina.

Wheat production is the third rural mainstay, but irrigation is playing a big part in a new look in agriculture—with products like cotton, sorghum and rice joining the well-established cereal, fruit and sugar growing industries.

The country's 256,000 rural holdings have a total area of about 1,210,000,000 acres—about 60 percent of the total land area. More than 90 percent of the utilised land is, however, natural or relatively unimproved rough grazing land, due to lack of water or unsuitable soil or topography. In the five years ended 1968 farm income averaged about seven percent of national income. In an industrially developing country this share is declining, but rural industries remain predominant as earners of foreign exchange, bringing in 68 percent of export income. Main recipients of Australian exports are, in order, Japan, the United Kingdom and the United States of America.

Since the end of 1945 Australia's population has increased by more than 4,700,000, or 64 percent. At the end of 1968 the population stood at 12,173,000—almost equally male and female. The rapid population increase was due both to the continuation of the higher birth rate of the war years and the influx of new people through the extensive immigration programme. State and city population figures at June 30, 1968, were: New South Wales 4,430,200 (Sydney 2,646,600); Victoria 3,356,900 (Melbourne 2,319,700); Queensland 1,751,800 (Brisbane 813,800); South Australia 1,136,400 (Adelaide 794,300); Western Australia 930,800 (Perth 606,000); Tasmania 386,000 (Hobart 144,900); A.C.T. 117,200

(Canberra City 110,000); Northern Territory 64,000 (Greater Darwin 26,800).

Population density is four persons per square mile, reflecting the size of areas unsuited for settlement because of lack of rianfall. Heaviest density is Australian Capital Territory, with 124·8 persons per square mile, followed by Victoria with 38 and New South Wales 14. The mainly urban character of life is substantiated by the 1966 reckoning that 58 percent of the population lived in capital cities, 25 percent in smaller urban centres and 17 percent in rural areas.

Immigration has been a big feature of Australian development. Since World War II 3,008,403 arrivals to December 1968 have stimulated growth and helped to offset the slow down caused by the low birth rate of the 1930s. This is balanced however by departures in the period totalling 1,094,958.

The Australian work force was estimated in June 1969 at 5,150,000, or about 42 percent of the population. Three of every ten males in the work force are in manufacturing industry, with commerce, primary production and building construction the other principal industry groups.

For women manufacturing absorbs about a quarter of the workforce, and most of the remainder are in commerce, principally the retail trades. The occupational distribution of the work force at the 1966 census was broadly: rural 10 percent, clerical 15, administrative, executive and managerial 6; professional, technical and related 9; sales workers 8; craftsman, production-process workers and labourers 35; transport and communications 6; service, sport and recreation 9; others 2.

The rapid increase of population has neccessitated a tremendous building programme. From 1947 to 1968 1,870,000 new houses and flats were completed—a new house or flat erected for every 2·5 persons added to the population in that time. Seven of every ten Australian homes are either owned or being bought by installment.

The Australian Government provides a comprehensive social security system, which includes health services, pensions for aged, invalids and widows, child endowment and unemployment and sickness benefits.

Since 1901 Australia has been a Federation of six States with the Federal Government responsible for national issues—external affairs, fiscal policy, broad-scale development, defence, trade and industry. The six States have more regional responsibilities—such as education, power, water, road building and transport, law enforcement, forestry and public works.

It is a stable system of Government which has been the essential background to growth, to the attainment of a high standard of living, to security, opportunity and a bright future.

DARWIN
Katherine
Wyndham
Derby
Broome
Tennant Cre
NORTH
TERRIT
Port Hedland
Dampier
Onslow
Alice Spring
Mt. Tom Price
Shark Bay
Carnarvon
WESTERN AUSTRALIA
Geraldton
Kalgoorlie
PERTH
Fremantle
Albany